MW01118271

ISBN: 9781290728362

Published by:
HardPress Publishing
8345 NW 66TH ST #2561
MIAMI FL 33166-2626

Email: info@hardpress.net
Web: http://www.hardpress.net

THE HUMANE IDEA

THE
HUMANE IDEA

A BRIEF HISTORY OF MAN'S ATTITUDE TOWARD THE OTHER ANIMALS, AND OF THE DEVELOPMENT OF THE HUMANE SPIRIT INTO ORGANIZED SOCIETIES

BY

FRANCIS H. ROWLEY

PRESIDENT OF THE MASSACHUSETTS SOCIETY FOR THE
PREVENTION OF CRUELTY TO ANIMALS
AND OF THE
AMERICAN HUMANE EDUCATION SOCIETY

Are not two sparrows sold for
a farthing? and not one of
them shall fall on the ground
without your Father.— Jesus

BOSTON
AMERICAN HUMANE EDUCATION SOCIETY
1912

IF THIS LITTLE VOLUME WERE WORTHY A PLACE BESIDE
THEIR FIDELITY AND DEVOTION, IT WOULD BE
DEDICATED TO TWO HORSES AND TWO DOGS TO
WHOSE COMPANIONSHIP AND INFLUENCE
THE AUTHOR OWES MORE THAN THE
STRANGER WOULD BELIEVE

CONTENTS

All animals are living hieroglyphs.
The dashing dog, and stealthy stepping cat,
Hawk, bull, and all that breathe, mean something more
To the true eye than their shapes show; for all
Were made in love and made to be beloved.
Thus must he think as to earth's lower life,
Who seeks to win the world to thought and love.

PHILIP JAMES BAILEY

THE PURPOSE

. . .

MY purpose in this small volume is to
be of service, particularly to the ordinary
humane worker. Scattered over the country are many deeply interested in the
cause that has for its aim the prevention
of cruelty to animals and the fostering
of such a sentiment as will ultimately
make prosecution for cruelty unnecessary.
Not a few of these workers are called upon
from time to time to speak upon some
phase of the subject. Often they are far
from public libraries where such books
might be obtained as those which would
be of assistance to them. It has seemed
to me that a brief, yet general survey of
the history of the humane idea would be
found useful.

It was Mr. Henry S. Salt's "Animals'
Rights," which I read many years ago,
that first indicated to me the direction in
which to look for material upon this theme.
To Mr. Salt I am much indebted, not only
for what he has so effectively done himself, but for the names of authors to whom
he has called attention. To the Countess
Cesaresco I am also under no little obligation. Her work entitled "The Place of

Animals in Human Thought" has been
of especial service to me.[1] Wherever I
have come upon any one with information
to offer upon our topic I have freely availed
myself of it.

It has been difficult to keep within the
narrow limits to which I have tried to confine myself. So many phases of the subject have been left untouched, so much
excluded that might have been written,
that the incompleteness of what I have
attempted can be no more evident to
anyone else than it is to me.

[1] In her "Outdoor Life in Greek and Roman Poets,"
there will also be found many interesting references to
fondness for animals on the part of ancient Greeks and
Romans, especially among those who sought pleasure in
the pursuits of agriculture.

THE HUMANE IDEA

Yet I doubt not through the ages one increasing purpose runs,
And the thoughts of men are widen'd with the process of the suns.   TENNYSON

THE attempt is made in this little book to trace, as briefly as possible, the history of that humane sentiment, particularly with reference to animals, out of which has grown at last the multitude of organizations that, in our modern day, not only seek to defend God's lowlier creatures from man's inhumanity, but to widen still further the spirit that unceasingly pleads for the just and kindly treatment of all sentient life. Man's relation to man, as well as his relation to other animals, falls within the circle of that spirit as it finds expression in what is slowly coming to be known as — humane education.

The study is a fascinating one and broadens under investigation till one finds himself led out into many lands, and set face to face with the history, the literature, the art, and the religions of mankind.

1

Of all the beasts he learned the language,
Learned their names and all their secrets,
How the beavers built their lodges,
Where the squirrels hid their acorns,
How the reindeer ran so swiftly
Why the rabbit was so timid,
Talked with them whene'er he met them,
Called them "Hiawatha's Brothers."

LONGFELLOW

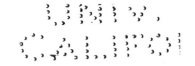

PRIMITIVE MAN

..

THE story even of primitive man, so far as we can fashion it, is not without interest to the student who follows back the trail in this realm of life. Our earliest ancestors, it seems very probable in the light of what we know, were far less in need of humane societies than we are. That they were not at first hunters and slayers of their humbler brethren of earth and air I think we are warranted in believing. Such other forms of life besides their own, as those which, under the influence of domestication, came to share with them their lot, were cherished, it is supposed, as friends and helpers. Probably only as the race moved toward cooler climates, or as great climatic changes transformed some sunnier land into one of snow and ice, did man find himself compelled to kill the furry creatures of the wild to clothe himself in their skins, or to supply himself with their flesh for food. It was necessity, may we not believe, that at first forced him into his carnivorous habits.

Some may recall Ovid's words, perhaps more scientific than once imagined, with reference to the Golden Age:

3

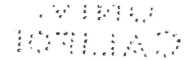

"We, by destroying life our life sustain,
 And gorge the ungodly man with meats obscene.
 Not so the Golden Age, which fed on fruit,
 Nor durst with bloody meals its mouth pollute." [1]

All this, however, was long before the time of the earliest man of whom we have any definite knowledge. Yet even this ancestor of ours who hunted and killed was a keen observer of animal life as his drawings of horse and reindeer on bits of bone, unearthed centuries after, bear witness.

[1] See "Outdoor Life in Greek and Roman Poets," (Countess Evelyn Martinengo-Cesaresco), chap. IX, p. 166, for evidences of Ovid's love for animals. With reference to animal sacrifices he says: "But what didst thou, O ox, and what did ye, O gentle sheep, to deserve a like fate?"

Also "The Animals' Cause," published by the Animal Defence and Antivivisection Society, London, 1909, p. 362.

THE HEBREW

. *. .

His tender mercies are over all His works.

A Psalmist

IF we begin with the Jewish scriptures not a few golden sayings will be recalled that tell of this spirit working in the soul of ancient Israel. Of course, reply may be made at once that the whole system of animal sacrifices goes far to refute any special regard for animal life during a long period of Jewish history. It may be said, however, that many hold — they believe with entire reason — that for that appalling institution of bloodshed which was a part of Israelitish worship there was no actual divine sanction; that we must see here the persistence of traditional customs and the influence of a priestly order with ends to subserve that were widely different from those great moral goals which rose before the inspired visions of the prophets. One must not forget the significance of Jeremiah's words (7: 22), "For I spake not unto your fathers, nor commanded them in the day that I brought them out of the land of Egypt, concerning burnt offerings or sacrifices; but this thing commanded I them, saying, Obey my

5

voice, and I will be your God, and ye shall be my people." [1]

Then we recall such positive sayings as, "Thou shalt not muzzle the ox when he treadeth out the corn"; [2] "Six days shalt thou do thy work, and on the seventh day shalt thou rest, that thine ox and thine ass may rest, etc."; [3] "Thou shalt not seethe a kid in his mother's milk"; [4] "The righteous man regardeth the life of his beast." [5] Many similar utterances could be quoted if space permitted. Our societies for the protection of children and animals might indeed, if they wished, go back to the days of the old Hebrew prophet, Jonah, for a divine sanction of their existence. The foolish heart of the ungracious preacher, you remember, was bidden contemplate what the destruction of Nineveh would mean to helpless children (the "six score thousand that did not discern between their right hand and their left"), and "much cattle." [6] All will recall Isaiah's vision of that holy mountain in which there is nothing to hurt or to destroy.[7]

[1] See Hastings' Bible Dictionary, Vol. IV, article on "Sacrifice"; also "The Prophecies of Jeremiah," C. J. Hall, p. 165.   [2] Deuteronomy xxv, 4.

[3] Exodus xxiii, 12.   [4] Exodus xxiii, 19.

[5] Proverbs xii, 10.   [6] Jonah iii, 11.

[7] For a similar prophetic vision, much discussed as to its interpretation, see the "Fourth Eclogue" of Vergil.

THE GREEK

.˙.

Yet dying as he was and almost drained of blood, he brought back the King from the midst of the foe, . . . and when he had carried him beyond weapon range he fell down on the spot and . . . breathed his last almost, as it were, with the consolation of human feeling. Then King Alexander, when he had gained the victory, founded a city on that site, and in honor of his horse called it Bucephala.

AULUS GELLIUS

GREECE, too, bears her witness to the prevalence of this spirit as in many ways touching into softer, fairer colors her marvelous life. True, her Homeric heroes feasted on many a slain victim of field and stall, when "The heralds brought a sacred hecatomb to the gods through the city, and the long-haired Grecians were assembled under the shady grove of far-darting Apollo." But, it has been said, "the ghost of a scruple had to be laid before the feast could be enjoyed." They had no butchers, these early Hellenes. They or their priests slew with their own hands the devoted animals.[1] The element of sacrifice seems to have been present everywhere as a sort of apology to

[1] "The Iliad," Bk. XIX, l, 253.

7

the victim whose flesh was afterward to be eaten.   The Iliad and the Odyssey both show us an almost modern attitude held by not a few toward the creatures that were man's faithful helpers.   The ox that plowed his fields, the horse that carried him in battle, — these were prized and loved by many of Homer's bravest and best.

The following lines I have found quoted from the Greek poet Addaeus Macedonis:

> "Alkon's ox is worn and old,
>   It has gained him grain and gold;
>   Must it to the shambles go?
>   'Nay,' says Alkon, 'never so.
>   Long he helped me at the plough,
>   I'll be grateful to him now —
>   His declining days shall pass
>   Knee deep in the pleasant grass.' " [1]

This might have been written yesterday, so truly does it represent many a modern man's thought toward some loyal four-footed servant.   No one who has ever read the Odyssey can forget the dog Argus, the sole friend of wandering Ulysses, that, old, neglected, dying, still recognized the returning pilgrim.   This is the picture the great artist sketches in half a dozen lines:

> "A dog was lying near,
> And lifted up his head and pricked his ears.

[1] See Palatine Anthology.

'Twas Argus, which the much enduring man
Ulysses long before had reared, but left
Untried, when for the hallowed town of Troy
He sailed. . . . And when he saw
Ulysses drawing near, he wagged his tail
And dropped his ears, but found that he could come
No nearer to his master, . . .
Ulysses, absent now for twenty years." [1]

In their games, the chariot race was not
only the favorite sport, but was thought of
as a religious event, and the horses parti-
cipating in the triumph shared the glory
conferred upon their owners. "For many
centuries," Plutarch tells us, "the graves
of Cimon's mares, with which he had thrice
conquered at the Olympian games, were
pointed out to the stranger, near his own
tomb." [2] The Athenians even inflicted
a fine, we read, on some heartless monster
who skinned a goat alive.[3] "Wanton
cruelty to animals," it has been written,
and I think justly, "seemed to the Greeks
an outrage to the gods."

Herodotus, in a story quoted by Lecky,
represents the sparrows that nested under

[1] "The Odyssey," Bk. XVII, ll. 291–327.
[2] Montaigne's "Essays," close of chap. LXVIII.
The statement is also made in this connection that
Xanthippus "caused his dog to be interred on an eminence
near the sea, which has ever since retained the name."
[3] "The Place of Animals in Human Thought," Countess
Martinengo-Cesaresco, p. 30.

the porticos of the temples, as the guests of the gods; and Aelian is reported by Lecky as saying that the Athenians condemned to death a boy for killing a sparrow that had taken refuge in the temple of Aesculapius.[1] We all recall the Hebrew singer's exquisite lines:

"Yea, the sparrow hath found an house
   And the swallow a nest for herself where she may lay her
       young,
   Even thine altars, O Lord of Hosts
   My King, and my God." [2]

The influence of Pythagoras' (died 496 B C?) teaching with reference to transmigration deserves more attention than we have time to give. It may at least be said that there are those who have ventured the suspicion that his hidden motive in the promulgation of the doctrine of reincarnation was to make men more humane. That this was the effect of his life and work will scarcely be questioned.

Aristotle's "On the Parts of Animals" has still interest for the philozoist. "Man and the mule," he remarks, "are always tame." We may not like the grouping, but he might have said a worse thing about us. The mule is a much maligned creature. He is no fool, as the old colored man inti-

[1] Lecky's "European Morals," Vol. II, p. 163.
[2] Psalm lxxxiv.

mated when he said: "I have learned if you have anything to say to a mule, you better say it to his face." Except in the senses of touch and taste, Aristotle held we are far surpassed by the other animals. Though he affirmed that only man, in the proper sense of the word, has the power of reason, he found in animals evident traces of a moral disposition.[1] He recognizes in them foresight, skill in meeting difficult situations that suddenly arise, and a strange power often of anticipating changes in wind and weather. With many others, we should not hesitate to differ with this great Greek authority concerning the animal's inability to reason. When a dog stands on the bank of a stream, prepares to jump, runs farther up where the stream is narrower, looks, hesitates, then goes still farther up to a yet narrower place before making the leap; we wonder how that mental act differs from our own in deciding whether it is safe to attempt to spring over a brook where it is six feet wide or whether we would not better follow up the bank and try it where we felt much surer of not slipping back or landing in the water.

[1] See "On the Parts of Animals," Bk. II, chap. X. "For of all living beings with which we are acquainted, man alone partakes of the divine, or, at any rate, partakes of it in a fuller measure than the rest."

On the whole, in spite of the exceptions that confront us in Greek history and literature, and notwithstanding the attitude of contempt in which so largely the Greeks regarded the world outside their own borders, and their system of slavery, the Greeks were in many respects responsive to the influence of the humane spirit, and did much to enlarge its power.[1]

Both Plutarch and Pliny the Elder are authorities for the following interesting story that reveals something of the sensitiveness of ancient Greece to the claims of this spirit: "When Pericles was building the Parthenon, a great number of mules were employed in drawing the stones up the hill of the Acropolis. Some of them became too old for the work, and these were set at liberty to pasture at large. But one old mule gravely walked every day to the stone yard and accompanied, or rather led, the procession of mule carts to and fro. The Athenians were delighted with its devotion to duty and decided that it should be supported at the expense of the state

[1] When it was suggested once that certain cruel sports, in imitation of the Roman spectacles, should be introduced into Athens, we are told that one opposing it said, in his address to the people, "Men of Athens, before you pass this motion, do not forget to destroy the Altar of Pity."

See Henry S. Salt's "Humanitarianism: Its General Principles and Progress."

for the rest of its days." [1] According to Pliny, the mule of the Parthenon lived till it had attained its eightieth year, "a record," it has been cleverly observed, "that seems startling even having regard to the proverbial longevity of pensioners." Suppose the story but a legend, which we have no reason to do, even then, that the legend arose, is evidence of the existence of a regard for man's humble servants that we had hardly expected to find so far away. Among the many shrines that forced the Christian apostle to say, "I perceive, O men of Athens, that ye are very religious," was one consecrated to Compassion.

[1] "The Place of Animals in Human Thought," Countess Martinengo-Cesaresco, pp. 66–67.

THE ROMAN

. . .

The birds in airy space might safely move,
And timorous hares on heaths securely rove;
Nor needed fish the guileless hook to fear.

OVID

WE enter a different atmosphere when we pass into the Roman world. "Who could imagine," an author writes, "Pericles presiding over a Roman holiday?" To dwell upon the cruel and bloody sports of the Roman arena is entirely unnecessary. Lecky says that in a single day at the dedication of the Colosseum by Titus, five thousand animals perished.[1] There must have been big game hunters and trappers then as now, justifying their barbarous cruelties, if not on scientific grounds, as in our day, then on the ground of the profit to be gained. Under Trajan the games continued for one hundred and twenty-three consecutive days. These atrocities, however, it should be said, did not characterize the earlier history of Rome. Prior to the year 186 B.C. there is no record of such bloodthirsty cruelties as in later times furnished amusement for the pleasure-

---

[1] Lecky's "European Morals," Vol. I, p. 280.

loving crowds that thronged to the Colosseum, where wealth and fashion, and extravagance gone mad, reveled in scenes that seem to us incredible.[1]

Still we are forced to believe that even in the Rome of those inhumane days there were innumerable exceptions to the all too common disregard of the sufferings of men and animals. Behind those few finer spirits whose names and writings add such luster to the annals of the empire there must have been a great company of kindly souls who found in teachers like Plutarch (b. 46 A.D.), Seneca (4 B.C. — 65 A.D.), and Porphyry (233–305), voices that uttered thoughts and feelings their own souls could share.[2] In his essay

[1] Yet are not the destruction, in modern times, of our birds of rare plumage, our merciless butchery of the seal, our inhuman methods of slaughtering our food animals, our prize fights, war, and, in America, our lynchings, quite as serious a reproach to our civilization when one thinks of the Christian centuries behind us?

[2] The Countess Cesaresco makes this very evident in her studies of the Greek and Roman poets. There was another side to the life of multitudes in what we call pagan times than that which has been vividly pictured by many writers anxious to deepen the contrast between the ages before Christianity and those that followed its advent. The spirit of Christianity has always been molding human life from the day of man's first appearance.

See also Cicero's letter to Marcus Marius (56 B.C.), quoted in Alfred Austin's autobiography, Vol. I, p. 120, "What pleasure can a cultivated man have, when either a helpless

on "Clemency" Seneca portrays to us a compassion toward all life that shows how deeply his character had been influenced by Sotio, his master, who was a disciple of Pythagoras and who taught a sacred regard for all living creatures whether in the human realm or below it.[1]

Porphyry, in his treatise "On Abstinence from Animal Food," writes words that are worthy to be placed beside the latest utterances of the most modern humanitarians. He says:

"Justice was not introduced from the alliance of men to each other, but justice consists in abstaining from injuring anything which is not noxious. Therefore since justice consists in not injuring anything, it must be extended as far as to every animated nature. He who is led by reason does not confine harmless conduct to men alone, but extends it to other animals and is so more similiar to divinty."[2] In the same Book he says: "If, however, it be requisite to speak the truth, not only reason may be perceived in all animals, but in many of them it is so great as to approximate to perfection." These last words recall the saying of Darwin: "We have seen that the senses and intuitions,

man is torn to pieces by a sanguinary beast, or a splendid animal is transfixed by a hunting spear."

[1] See essay on "Clemency," Bohn's Classical Library.
[2] Porphyry on "Abstinence from Food," Bk. III.

the various emotions and faculties, such as love, memory, attention, curiosity, imitation, reason, etc., of which man boasts, may be found in an incipient, or even sometimes in a well-developed condition, in the lower animals." [1]

In the light of the latest conclusions of science are we not returning to an earlier and truer conception of the unity of all life, and to a brotherhood wider than that which has been the theme of much of our Christian theology?

But of all these choice souls Plutarch is the one pre-eminently to whom we turn as the teacher of his day and worthy to be ranked with the leaders of recent times who have been recognized as most imbued with the spirit of a great humanity. While evidences of his gentle temper appear in his "Lives," it is in the far less well known "Moralia" that he is seen as the friend and champion of that wide world of life below us. There he has three essays devoted to animals. They are, "On Eating of Flesh," "Which are the most Crafty, Water Animals or those Creatures that tread upon the Land?" and "That Brute Beasts Reason." [2] "It is the voice of the highly civilized Greek," says the Countess Cesa-

[1] "Descent of Man," chap. III.

[2] Plutarch's "Moralia," Prof. William W. Goodwin's translation, Vol. V.

resco, "addressing the young barbarians of Rome."

The essays delight you with their wise moderation. He never allows his feelings to carry him into wild or extravagant assertions. Always under self-control, always dignified, calm, patient, not seeking to force agreement with himself when there may be just ground for a difference of opinion, he nevertheless, with utmost frankness and sincerity, stands forth the unswerving friend of the defenseless animals, and pleads for them on the ground of a universal benevolence and a wide justice that make his words sound almost as if written yesterday. Though averse to eating flesh, he refuses to denounce you if you are not a vegetarian. "Be as humane as you can," he says. "Cause as little suffering as possible. Let us eat flesh if we must, but for hunger, not self-indulgence. If we kill animals we must still be compassionate, not heaping outrages and tortures, as, alas is done every day." "When we take our recreation," he writes, "those who help us in the fun ought to share in it and be amused as well." "With him cruelty to animals does not lie in the use but in the abuse of them," says one summarizing his opinions; "it is not cruel to kill them if they are incompatible with our own existence, it is not cruel to tame or train to our service those made by nature gentle and loving toward man which become the companions of his toil according to their natural aptitude." "The Stoics," he writes, "made sensibility toward animals a preparation to humanity and compassion because the gradually formed habit of the lesser affections is capable of leading men very far."

Take the following from his "Marcus Cato": "Kindness and beneficence should be extended to creatures of every species, and these still flow from the breast of a well-natured man as streams that issue from the living fountain. A good man will take care of his horses and dogs, not only when they are young, but when old and past service." "We certainly ought not," he continues, "to treat living creatures like shoes or household goods, which when worn out with use, we throw away, and were it only to teach benevolence to human kind, we should be merciful to other creatures. For my own part I would not sell even an old ox."

Of Plutarch, Lecky says, "He places the duty of kindness to animals on the broad ground of the affections, and he urges that duty with an emphasis and a detail to which no adequate parallel can, I believe, be found in the Christian writings for at least seventeen hundred years."[1]

[1] Lecky's "European Morals," Vol. II, p. 166.

OTHER LANDS

. .

Nay let me lose such glory; for its sake
I would not leave one living thing I loved.
. . . not for Swarga's bliss
Quit I Mahendra, this poor clinging dog.

"Idylls of India," SIR EDWIN ARNOLD

EGYPT, Persia, India, the lands that own the faith of Mohammed, indeed the entire Orient, offers much to the student of man's relation to the animal world. Into this wide field I do not even attempt a glance. In general it may be said that, all things considered, animals probably have received a kinder treatment in far Eastern countries than in the Occident. The doctrine of reincarnation has doubtless been influential here, but outside of this the spirit of Eastern civilization in many ways is of a gentler type than that which has characterized the life of the Western world.[1] The West has been described by more than one Oriental as "the hell of animals."

The Jainas will kill nothing. They will not eat flesh of any kind. And this

[1] Sir Edwin Arnold's "Idylls of India," "The Hound of Yudhishthira."

not because of their transmigration ideas
merely, but because, they affirm, of kindness and humanity. This last statement
I know is seriously questioned by competent scholars. The Buddhist will not
kill that he may eat, but if an animal is
dead and the life gone, "why," he says,
"shall I not eat its flesh?"

In the face of all that has been taught in
India by these two systems, I have read
very recently a paper,[1] by a humane officer
in Bengal, which charges upon that country an amount of cruelty in the treatment
of animals that makes one wonder if it
can be the land of Buddha and Mahavira.

Somewhere I saw the statement that
whatever is said of the treatment of animals
in the East, this at least is true, that the
children are not cruel. Travelers in Japan
report a regard for animals as well as for
children that stands in marked contrast
with much of what is true in Europe and
America.

[1] "The Animals' Cause" (published by the Animal
Defence and Antivivisection Society, London), p. 316.

EARLY CHRISTIANITY

. . .

So the wild birds were tamed by love alone,
And dwelt with Francis in his convent home.

AXON

AMONG the puzzling questions that arise in tracing the development of the humane idea is that connected with the apparent indifference of early Christianity with regard to the value of subhuman life. The fault was not, certainly, in the spirit or teachings of the founder of the Christian faith. No more wonderful word was ever spoken with reference to man's attitude toward all sentient life below him, or with more wide-reaching significance in this direction, than the saying of Jesus which tells us that not even a sparrow can fall to the ground without our Father. If the Infinite and the Eternal marks the death of so frail and fleeting a being as a sparrow, how can we be the children of our Father in heaven and not bear toward bird and beast the relationship of elder brothers, guarding them against all injustice and needless suffering?

St. Paul, influenced here no doubt by the prevailing Jewish thought of his day with reference to animals, failed to see in the old Hebrew prohibition against muzzling the ox that threshed the corn, any divine care for oxen; that was something quite unworthy the great God.[1]   There is a St. Paul Humane Society, but it is named after St. Paul of Minnesota and not of Tarsus or Jerusalem.   Where else, however, did the mighty heart of St. Paul fail in its almost divine sympathies and compassion?   Surely we can forgive him this.

The answer to the question, why the Church for so many centuries practically ignored the claims of the animal world is too many-sided to be more than outlined. In the first place the value placed upon the individual human soul by Christianity was supreme, and the vast importance of its salvation was naturally held to be the all-absorbing duty of the Church.   This dwarfed every other consideration.   Of what value are the beasts that, it was taken for granted, perish, compared with the one and only thing of moment — immortal man?

Beyond this, and perhaps as scarcely less determining, is the fact, called to our attention by a modern writer, that two of the pronounced critics of early Christianity were Celsus (first half first century) and Porphyry, writers sharing in ideas of the

[1] I Corinthians ix, 9 — 10.

animal world that savored of oriental and pagan cults.[1]

Both these men were worthy antagonists of the early faith — Celsus, a man of vast learning and wide knowledge of historic religions; and Porphyry, known as *the* philosopher, the most learned thinker of his time. "Celsus appears to have inclined," says this writer, "toward the theory that the soul, life, mind, only, is made by God, the corruptible and passing body being a natural growth or perhaps the handiwork of inferior spirits. He denied that reason belonged to man alone, and still more strongly that God created the universe for man rather than for other animals — only absurd pride, he affirms, can engender such a thought. He knew very well that this, far from being a new idea, was the normal view of the ancient world from Aristotle to Cicero. He takes Euripides to task for saying, — 'The sun and moon are made to serve mankind.' Why mankind? he asks; why not ants and flies? Night serves them also for rest and day for seeing and working. As to ants, he says, they practise the science of social economy just as well as we do; they have granaries which they fill with provisions for the

[1] "The Place of Animals in Human Thought," Countess Martinengo-Cesaresco, p. 339.

winter; they help their comrades if they see them bending under the weight of a burden; they carry their dead to places which become family tombs; they address each other when they meet; whence it follows that they never lose their way. We conclude, therefore, that they must have complete reasoning powers and common notions of general truths, and that they have a language and know how to express fortuitous events." [1]

Porphyry, we have seen, held to very much the same ideas concerning animal life. "It could not have been," says the writer recently quoted, "a fortunate coincidence that two of the most prominent men who held these ideas in the early centuries were declared foes of the new faith." In combating them the early Fathers may have been unduly led to ignore the value of all life below the human. That the more eastern and pagan faiths gave a larger place in their thought to the subhuman world of life, I feel personally convinced, had something to do with the seeming disregard of the whole subject by the Fathers.

Here at least is the fact that for centuries the Church remained steadily indifferent to the claims of the lower animals; and, — save for such exceptions as St. Francis

---

[1] See Mæterlinck's "The Life of the Bee."

of Assisi (1182–1226), and the experiences of a host of saintly anchorets which gave rise to many a legend of animal intelligence and companionship, and the animal symbols used of Christ, like the lamb, the panther, and others, — exerted no influence to inculcate the spirit of any just consideration for them.

Perhaps this ought not to surprise us, for, even down to our own day, it can hardly be said that the ministry of the Christian church as a whole sustains any vital relation to the great humane movement. There are splendid exceptions, but, to the vast majority of them, the care and consideration given to animals seems rather the work of men and women more or less odd, to say the least. This, at any rate, we are compelled to say as the result of our experience — and it is an experience that entitles us to speak with some degree of assurance — that, directly, the pulpit has not been, as an institution, a very serious helper of our humane societies.

THE DAWNING OF THE NEW DAY

. . .

The year's at the Spring,
The day's at the morn.

BROWNING

WE wait till the time of the revival of learning before we begin again to hear, save here and there, any voice that clearly intimates that animals have rights that man is bound to respect. Leonardo da Vinci, 1452–1519, and Montaigne, 1533–1592, and Giordano Bruno, 1548–1600, all left behind them sayings that remind one of Plutarch and Porphyry, but they were the exceptions.[1] The humanist was by no means always the humanitarian.

Slowly, however, in that period marked by many a fierce spirit of cruelty and brutal inhumanity does the humane sentiment rise into recognition. Still it is not until

---

[1] Montaigne's "Essays," chap. LXVIII, "Of Cruelty." "There is a certain natural commerce and mutual obligation between them (the animals) and us." See also chap. LXIX for many references to animals.

we come into the eighteenth century that
the evidences appear in the recorded utterances of leaders of thought that men's
consciences are seriously awakening to
their duties to their humbler fellow-creatures.   Voltaire and Rousseau were fore-
most spirits of that period which began to
see with nobler vision the larger things that
opened before humanity.   It was Rousseau
who, no matter what we say of his strange
life, said, "O men be humane! It is your
first duty.   What wisdom can there be for
you without humanity?"[1]   "From the
great Revolution of 1789," says Henry S.
Salt, "dates the period when the world-
wide spirit of humanitarianism, which had
hitherto been felt by but one man in a
million — the thesis of the philosopher or
the vision of the poet — began to disclose
itself, gradually and dimly at first, as an
essential feature of democracy."[2]

Leaving untouched the doctrine of Des-
cartes which ranked the lower animals as
mere automata, without sensibility or
capacity for pain — a teaching which un-
doubtedly had much to do with retard-
ing the development in many quarters

[1] For Rousseau's fondness for animals see his "Second
Dialogue."
Whether we translate these words "O men be humane,"
or "O men be human," it matters not for the thought.
[2] See Henry S. Salt's "Animals' Rights," p. 4.

of a juster conception of animal life; passing by Schopenhauer's opposition to this teaching of the Cartesian School, in his "Foundation of Morality,"[1] we turn to the England of the eighteenth century to find the marked leaders of this later day in the realm of the humanitarian movement so far as animals are concerned.

There are many names that deserve attention, but we tarry to mention only a few. There was John Hildrop, 1742, author of "Free Thought upon the Brute Creation." The Rev. Dr. Humphrey Primatt, also, 1776, whose "Dissertation on the Duty of Mercy and the Sin of Cruelty to Brute Animals" is a strong plea for justice and humanity. We select the following from one of his volumes:

"And for the same reason (that is, because a man would consider it unjust to cause another man unnecessary pain) he will not torment or abuse a brute, but will consider that the meanest creature upon earth, if it be in no respect harmful to him, has an equal right with him to enjoy the blessings of life."

"The many horrid instances of cruelty practised by men . . . would almost tempt one to think that a great part of

[1] For translation of a remarkable passage see Mr. Howard Williams' "Ethics of Diet."

mankind believed that cruelty to brutes is not an act of injustice. It is certain, however, that the cruelty of men to brutes is a greater act of injustice than the cruelty of men to men."

He then proceeds to show that animals have the following rights: The right to food, to rest and to tender usage at the hands of men, for he says, "These things the goodness of their Creator has been pleased to covenant for on their behalf and to enjoin by His written law." This he shows by the words which "forbid the thresher to muzzle the ox," by the command, "the cattle shall have rest on the Sabbath day," and by the quotation, a "righteous man will regard the life of his beast."

He laments that so few parents instruct children to treat animals kindly. Of allowing children to be cruel, he says, "Such indulgence roots out from their once tender hearts every feeling of pity and compassion, so true is it that our treatment of beasts has an influence on our moral character." [1]

He advocates the Golden Rule as our law for the treatment of animals.

Soame Jenyns (1704–1787), essayist and poet, wrote on "Cruelty to Inferior

[1] "The Book of Nature," Toogood, Boston, 1802, to which is added, p. 37, Primatt's Dissertation.

Animals." [1]   These are some of the finer
souls who prepared the way for better
known successors and for the larger day
into which we have entered.

Among such, during the latter part of
the eighteenth and the beginning of the
nineteenth century, was Jeremy Bentham,
scholar and jurist, who first advocated
legal measures for the protection of animals, asserting that as "slaves have been
treated by the law exactly upon the same
footing as, in England, for example, the
inferior races of animals are still, yet the
day may come when the rest of the animal
creation may acquire those rights which
could never have been withholden from
them but by the hand of tyranny."

Of Bentham, C. M. Atkinson, one of
his biographers, says: — "Bentham insisted that acts of cruelty to animals must
be classed among crimes or offenses cog-
nizable by law; the word *crime*, said he,
being incurably indistinct and ambiguous,
is the word to be employed on all rhetorical
occasions. He foretold the coming of a
time when humanity shall stretch her
mantle over everything which breathes."

"Why, he asked, should the law refuse
its protection or deny its aid to any sensi-

[1] We have been pleased to discover that Jenyns not
only wrote upon this topic, but against the taxation of
the American colonies by Great Britain.

tive being? With characteristic vigor he urged the suppression of all forms of wilful cruelty." [1]

It is exceedingly interesting, so far back from our present time, to have him quoted as "contending that the death of animals may be rendered less painful by the adoption of many simple processes well worthy of being studied." Here is a prevision of those more humane methods of slaughter that are slowly taking possession of the minds of men. Bentham also insisted that "if humanity to animals — the sentiment of benevolence — were inculcated in the minds of children, it would tend toward the prevention of crimes of violence." [2]

Here again he is in entire harmony with the latest humanitarians. His biographer has called attention to the fact that the distinguished painter, Hogarth, "in tracing cruelty through its different stages had represented it as beginning with delight in the suffering of animals, and ending in the most savage murder."

But Jeremy Bentham was ahead of his time. The world was not yet ready for legislation in defense of the animal. We wait till 1811 before another champion of the *jus animalium* appears with the pur-

[1] "Jeremy Bentham: His Life and Work," C. M. Atkinson, pp. 145–147.

[2] See Bentham's "Pity's Gift" (1798).

pose to embody it in the law of the land. Lord Erskine, in that year of grace, introduces into Parliament a bill for the legal protection of animals. In that august body, where noble lords of the realm, bishops of the Church of the All-Merciful sat in the seats of the mighty, his voice was drowned amid a wild tumult of hisses, catcalls, and laughter.

Ten years pass and once again a member of this same legislature rises to offer a bill in behalf of those who can never plead for themselves in any court of justice. This time it is Richard Martin of Galway, an Irishman, a man whom no ridicule or laughter can crush or cow. Mr. Martin, justly or unjustly, we cannot say, had acquired quite a reputation as a duelist. It is related that after having introduced his measure in Parliament and having returned to his seat, a startling wail broke out from someone behind him. This, it is supposed, was an attempt to imitate the cry of a cat and was evidently aimed in reproach at Martin. He rose from his seat and, with a look that few men cared to face, turned and very deliberately said, "Will the gentleman who has just spoken please stand up?" No one responding, Martin, addressing the Chair, said, "Mr. Speaker, if the gentleman who insulted me will send his card to the Clerk's desk, I will retire to a committee room and explain the bill to him." [1]   It is needless to say no card was forthcoming.

It needed an Irish heart, strong, brave, impulsive, yet tender and compassionate. Backed by a little group of kindred souls he forced through Parliament in 1822 the first legislation of modern times that promised legal protection for animals.   This bill is known as "Humanity Martin's Cattle Bill," and Richard Martin's name is written high on the scroll that bears the list of the great leaders in our cause.

It should be said that this Act of 1822 did not include by any means all animals. The bull and the dog were not protected from cruelty by its provisions.   When, however, in 1824 the English Society for the Prevention of Cruelty to Animals was founded, as the fruit of Martin's Bill, efforts were put forth for its amendment, resulting in securing in 1835 protection for the bull, the dog, and lamb, and prohibiting the baiting and fighting of dogs, bulls, bears, badgers, and cocks.[2]

Other and important amendments have been secured from time to time, the last having been obtained in 1911, which has considerably increased the power of the Royal Society.   Queen Victorie was a loyal supporter of the English S. P. C. A.

[1] "The Humane Movement," McCrea, p. 30.
[2] "The Humane Movement," McCrea, p. 31.

through her long reign.   Indeed, it was because of her interest and patronage that the title "Royal" was bestowed upon the organization.   In England the one great parent society is represented by many branches throughout the island.

AMERICA

. .

Let each new temple, nobler than the last,
Shut thee from heaven with a dome more vast.

HOLMES

WHEN we cross to our own shores we find that, long before any organized efforts were made in America toward the formation of societies for the prevention of cruelty to animals, there had been as in England notable pioneers in the field of humane sentiment and expression. The first, so far as we have been able to discover, was that distinguished advocate of so much that is distinctly American, Thomas Paine. In his "Age of Reason" he says:

"The moral duty of man consists in imitating the moral goodness and beneficence of God manifested in the creation toward all his creatures. . . . Everything of persecution and revenge between man and man, and everything of cruelty to animals is a violation of moral duty."

"The only idea we can have of serving God is that of contributing to the happiness of the living creation God has made." [1]

---

[1] "The Age of Reason," by Thomas Paine, edited by Moncure Daniel Conway, Part I, p. 83.

There is also in the *Pennsylvania Magazine* for May, 1775, a poem by him bearing the title, "Cruelty to Animals Exposed." The poem describes Paine's vigorous deliverance of a little kitten from the fate of being destroyed by dogs into the midst of which a "wretch" had thrown her. That he anticipated the need of slaughter-house reform seems evident by his description of a scene that met his eye as he followed the heartless possessor of the kitten to the place where he flung her among the dogs:

"Without the town, besmear'd with filth and blood,
And foul with stench, a common butch'ry stood;
Where sheep by scores unpitied fell a prey,
And lordly oxen groan'd their lives away;
Where village dogs, with half the dogs in town,
Contention held, and quarrel'd for a bone."

Still another early friend of animals appears in Samuel J. Pratt (1838), who, picturing the cruelties of slavery, portrays also the suffering of the subhuman world, calling attention particularly to the atrocities of the slaughter-house. The lines that follow are worth quoting:

"'Tis not enough that daily slaughter feeds,
That the fish leaves its stream, the lamb its meads,
That the reluctant ox is dragg'd along,
And the bird ravish'd from its tender song,
That in reward of all her music giv'n,

The lark is murder'd as she soars to Heaven:
'Tis not enough, our appetites require
That on their altars hecatombs expire;
But cruel man, with more than bestial power,
Must heap fresh horrors on life's parting hour:
Full many a being that bestows its breath,
Must prove the pang that waits a *ling'ring* death,
Here, close pent up, must gorge unwholesome food,
There, render drop by drop the smoking blood;
The quiv'ring flesh improves as slow it dies,
And Lux'ry sees th' augmented whiteness rise;
Some gashed and mangled feel the torturer's art,
Writhe in their wounds, tho' sav'd each vital part.
Ask you the cause? the *food more tender grows,*
And callous Lux'ry triumphs in the blows:
For this, are some to raging flames consign'd
While yet alive, to sooth our taste refin'd!
O power of mercy, that suspends the rod!
O shame to man, impiety to God!
Thou polish'd Christian, in the untutor'd see, .
The sacred right of sweet HUMANITY.
Thine is the World, thy crimson spoils enjoy,
But let no wanton arts thy soul employ;
Live, tho' thou dost on blood, ah! still refrain
To load thy victims with superfl'ous pain;
Ev'n the gaunt tiger, tho' no life he saves,
In generous *haste* devours what famine craves;
The bestial paw may check thy human hands,
And teach *dispatch* to what thy want demands,
Abridge thy sacrifice, and bid thy knife,
For HUNGER KILL, BUT NEVER SPORT WITH LIFE."

"Tyrants o'er brutes with ease extend the plan,
And rise in cruelty from beast to man:
Their sordid policy each crime allows,
The flesh that quivers and the blood that flows,

The furious stripes that murder in a day,
Or torturing arts that kill by dire delay;
The fainting spirit and the bursting vein,
All, all are reconcil'd to Christian gain." [1]

EARLY LEGISLATION

It is interesting to find that, some time before any organized movement in the direction of the prevention of cruelty to animals was begun in this country, three States, at least, had secured the passage of laws making possible to some degree, the protection of animals.   The first law that we have been able to discover is the following, which was passed by the legislature of New York State in 1829:

Section 26.   MAIMING AND CRUELTY TO ANIMALS. — Every person who shall maliciously kill, maim or wound any horse, ox or other cattle, or any sheep, belonging to another, or shall maliciously and cruelly beat or torture any such animal, whether belonging to himself or another, shall, upon conviction, be adjudged guilty of a misdemeanor.   Title 6, Part IV., Chapter 1, Section 26, Vol. II, page 695, of the Revised Statutes of the State of New York, January 1, 1829.

Massachusetts   comes   next,   with   a statute reported in 1834 by a commission

[1] "Humanity or Rights of Nature" (pamphlets on slavery), by S. J. Pratt.

appointed by the governor to revise the general statutes of the commonwealth, and this became operative in 1836:

"Every person who shall cruelly beat or torture any horse, ox or other animal, whether belonging to himself or another, shall be punished by imprisonment in the county jail for not more than one year or by fine not exceeding one hundred dollars.":

Section 22, Chap. 130, Revised Statutes of Mass. (1836).

In recommending this provision to the legislature the commissioners say in their report on the general statutes of the commonwealth (1834):

"It probably is not generally known in the community that extreme cruelty to animals even when inflicted by the owner is an offense punished by the common law. Almost every one must have witnessed very revoltable instances of such cruelty, particularly with regard to horses. There seems to be less excuse for the commission of this offense than most others; and the commissioners submit for the consideration of the legislature the expediency of adopting some reasonable provision on the subject."

At common law cruelty to animals was not an offense on the ground of the pain and suffering inflicted (People v. Brunell 48 How. Pr., N. Y., 435). But when the act was committed publicly and so as to constitute a nuisance, or when committed with a malicious intent to injure the owner it was indictable.

(Stage Horse cases 15 Abb. Pr. N.S., N. Y., 51; U. S. v. McDuell, 5 Cranch C. C. (U. S.) 391; People v. Brunell, *supra*.)

It was therefore in 1836 that cruelty to animals first became in Massachusetts a criminal offense on the ground of suffering and pain inflicted.

In 1855, Senator William A. Crabbe, of Pennsylvania, had drawn up and presented to the legislature of his State this statute:

AN ACT

To prevent and punish wanton cruelty to animals in the City of Philadelphia.

Section 1.   Be it enacted by the Senate and House of Representatives of the Commonwealth in General Assembly met, and it is hereby enacted by the authority of the same.

That from and after the passage of this act any person or persons who shall, in the City of Philadelphia, wantonly or cruelly maltreat, beat or otherwise abuse any animal or animals, belonging either to himself or to others, shall be deemed guilty of a misdemeanor, and shall be fined by any alderman of said city, for the first offense, in a sum not less than five dollars nor more than ten dollars, and for the second and every subsequent offense, in a sum not less than ten nor exceeding twenty dollars, to be paid to the guardians of the poor for the use of the said city: and if said fine or penalty be not paid, then said alderman shall commit said offender to the county prison, there to remain until discharged by due course of law, provided:

That when the fine imposed exceeds the sum of five dollars, the party complained against may appeal from the decision of said alderman to the court of quarter sessions, upon his entering bail in the nature of a recognizance in the usual manner, for his appearance at the said court, where the offense shall be prosecuted in the same manner as is now directed by law in such cases: And provided also, That the provisions of this act shall in no way interfere with the present common law remedy by indictment except when the party has been tried before an alderman as aforesaid, and the case not appealed from or returned to the court of quarter sessions.

Approved the third day of May, A.D. 1855.

JAMES POLLOCK.

Page 421 P.L. 1855.

Originally it was intended that this law should cover the entire state of Pennsylvania, but by reason of an amendment it was restricted to the city of Philadelphia.

HENRY BERGH

The first organized work, however, in behalf of animals in America was undertaken by the now widely known humanitarian, Henry Bergh.

Mr. Bergh was born in the city of New York in 1823. His father, who had been a successful shipbuilder, left him at his death a comfortable fortune. He was educated at Columbia College, having traveled some time in Europe before the completion of his college life. In 1862 he was appointed Secretary of the Legation at St. Petersburg and Acting Consul. It is there that he first became interested in the subject of prevention of cruelty to animals.

Upon his return to New York he devoted himself to awakening public sentiment on their behalf, and finally, as the result of his unremitting labor, there was passed, April 10, 1866, by the New York State Legislature, the act of incorporation of the American Society for the Prevention of Cruelty to Animals. On April 22, twelve days later, the Society was organized in Clinton Hall. Among the notable men who stood with Mr. Bergh in this movement were Peter Cooper, George Bancroft, the famous historian, and Horace Greeley.

At this time the only law with reference

to animal protection in New York State was one which, as already seen, was aimed at any person who "shall maliciously kill or wound any horse, ox, cattle or sheep belonging to himself or another, or who shall maliciously and cruelly beat any such animal belonging to himself or another." Nothing in this law was designed to cover such cruelties as were often practised upon a great multitude of food animals, nothing that protected the cat or dog, nothing that forbade the abandonment of a sick or injured animal, or leaving it to die from lack of food and exposure.

An interesting event in the early history of this Society has been told by one of Mr. Bergh's biographers as follows: "A benevolent Frenchman named Louis Bonard died and bequeathed his property to the Society. Mr. Bergh did not meet Mr. Bonard until just before his death when he was sent for to visit him at St. Vincent's Hospital. 'I have,' said the sick man, 'long entertained a deep regard for the Society for the Prevention of Cruelty to Animals and want to bequeath to it all my property.' The amount was more than one hundred thousand dollars. It has been said that this Mr. Bonard had made a large part of his fortune in the fur business and that it was a satisfaction to his conscience that he could thus in some way try to make recompense for the cruelty his business had necessitated."

It is a fact not generally known that it was also through Mr. Bergh's activities that the first society in the world for the protection of children from cruelty was founded.[1]   He died March 12, 1888.

I know of no more striking evidence of the progress of this cause in America than the fact that forty-two years after Henry Bergh, amid ridicule and contempt, founded the New York Society, there was established at Columbia University a chair on the "Henry Bergh Foundation for the Promotion of Humane Education."

CAROLINE EARLE WHITE

The organization of the second anti-cruelty society in the United States took place in Philadelphia.   At that time Mrs. Caroline Earle White, now, 1912, the President of the Women's Pennsylvania Society for the Prevention of Cruelty to Animals, was in the prime of her early womanhood.   By nature deeply interested in the animal world, she was led by reports of what was being done in New York to visit Mr. Bergh, that she might learn from him the methods he had adopted in forming the American Society.   She returned

[1] Bulletin of the American S. P. C. A. for February, 1912.

to her own city greatly stirred by the
interview and, single-handed, set about at
once securing the pledges of prominent
citizens to join in a movement to organize
a similar society in Philadelphia.   To this
lifelong champion of the animals' cause —
this noble and accomplished woman — is,
therefore, due the founding of the Pennsylvania Society in 1867.

George Thorndike Angell

Two years before Mr. Bergh had called
into being the American Society, Mr.
George T. Angell, of Boston, in 1864, had
by his will provided that in case of his
death a considerable portion of his property should be used for "circulating in the
schools and elsewhere information calcu-
lated to prevent cruelty to animals."   The
Massachusetts Society, however, founded
by Mr. Angell, was not organized until
March 31, 1868, the act of incorporation
having been obtained from the legislature
eight days previously.

George T. Angell, who founded the
Massachusetts Society for the Prevention
of Cruelty to Animals and the American
Humane Education Society (this latter
incorporated in 1889), was born in South-
bridge, Massachusetts, June 5, 1823.
Mr. Angell was educated at Brown University and Dartmouth College.   He

was admitted to the bar in December, 1851. After some years of successful practice, he gave up his chosen profession and devoted the remainder of his life, to the ripe age of eighty-six, to the furtherance of the work of the two Societies of which he was, from the beginning until his death, the president and the guiding genius.

To those who believe that underneath all this work of justice and kindness there lies a foundation of abiding faith in the eternal source of these virtues, there will be pleasure in reading the following from Mr. Angell's Autobiographical Sketches: "At the close of the meeting at which the Massachusetts Society for the Prevention of Cruelty to Animals was organized, Mr. Sturgis (just elected honorary secretary) went with me to my office underneath the hall; and with a deep sense of the great work we believed we had that day inaugurated, we knelt and asked God's blessing."[1] It is not too much to say that from its inception this Society has been administered in a reverent fear of God and with unfailing faith in the Eternal Goodness.

There is no doubt that Mr. Angell regarded the work of the American Humane Education Society as one destined to have a vastly wider influence as time goes on

[1] "Autobiographical Sketches," George T. Angell, p. 12.

than is possible to any society that exists chiefly for the prevention of cruelty to animals. The present activities of this organization, and the outlook for its future as an educational force in this and other lands, certainly justify his opinion.

"Our Dumb Animals"

Mr. Angell also, in June, 1868, within a few months of the organization of the Massachusetts S. P. C. A., began the publication of *Our Dumb Animals,* the first paper of its kind in the world. The circulation has grown remarkably from the beginning, until now it is nearly sixty-five thousand a month. That this paper has been one of the mightiest missionary forces in carrying far and wide into every nation under heaven the gospel of a large humanity no one familiar with its character and history can doubt.

Mr. Angell was also instrumental in the organization of the Illinois Humane Society. In 1870 he went to Chicago, engaged an office on Washington Street, and for the next four months labored incessantly, with the assistance of the Hon. John C. Dore and Edwin Lee Brown, for this purpose, the result being the formation of that Society in the year 1871. Among the names forever to be associated with the Illinois Society is that of Mr.

John G. Shortall, from 1892–1898 its honored president. It was to this courtly, distinguished, and accomplished humanitarian that the writer of these words owes, more than to any other, his interest in humane work.

Other societies for the prevention of cruelty to animals have followed from time to time in the several States of the Union until there are now something more than three hundred active organizations. Approximately the number for the entire world, as nearly as can be determined, is eight hundred.

The Band of Mercy Movement

The first Band of Mercy was organized in England, in 1875, by Catherine Smithies. Yet Mrs. Smithies was more than willing to share with Mr. Angell the honor connected with the organization of this remarkable movement that has spread almost, if not quite, around the world.[1] Mr. Angell had visited England some years before and while there had been very influential in arousing interest in various forms of humane work. Among the people he met was Catherine Smithies, who wrote him in December, 1875, referring to the Band of Mercy organization, "I do not

[1] "Autobiographical Sketches," George T. Angell, pp. 36, 78, 82.

forget that you were the means in God's
hand of beginning the Ladies' Society, one
fruit of which is the present one."

In July, 1882, just as Mr. Angell was
preparing for a campaign of humane education, and considering drawing up a
pledge card for the children of the public
schools, the Rev. Thomas Timmins, of
Portsmouth, England, came to this country. Mr. Timmins had been connected
with the English Band of Mercy. His
arrival seemed to Mr. Angell a veritable
providence. For many days they conferred over the project of an American
Band of Mercy which should be "different
from anything that had preceded it. It
should include all harmless living creatures, human and dumb. It should have
its own pledge, badge, and card of
membership."

The badge agreed upon was a five-
pointed star on which is engraved "Glory
to God," "Peace on Earth," "Good Will
to All," "Kindness to all Living Creatures." The pledge adopted was, "I will
try to be kind to all harmless living creatures, and try to protect them from cruel
usage." This has since been changed by
omitting the word "harmless." Even a
harmful creature one would protect from
cruel usage, and if he destroyed it, would
do it mercifully.

Among the first to identify themselves

with the parent band in Boston were the
Governor of Massachusetts, the Mayor of
Boston, the Roman Catholic Archbishop,
Chief Justice Morton of the Supreme
Court, and Wendell Phillips. Many other
distinguished citizens also became members. At the end of the first year there
were ninety-three organizations with about
ten thousand members. At the present
writing, 1912, there are 85,098, into which
have been gathered something more than
three million children.

The vast influence of this work it is
impossible to estimate. For thirty years
it has been reaching the children of our
public schools in every State of the Union.
Hosts of these are now men and women.
Temporary as the results may have been
in many cases, there is no doubt that
hundreds of thousands have felt the power
of its spirit and that their attitude toward
all sentient life has been changed by it.
Steadily, year after year, it has been
preaching its gospel of peace, brotherli-
ness, kindness, and good will. How large
a part it has played in arousing and fostering the peace sentiment in this country
(it has always been protesting against
war) no one can ever know.

These Bands of Mercy exist now in
nearly every civilized country of the world,
and are in more or less direct commu-
nication with the head office in Boston.

Indeed the great work in Cuba, under Mrs. Jeannette Ryder, with whom we constantly co-operate, is carried on by her Band of Mercy. Within the past two years hundreds of these bands have been organized in Turkey, South Africa, Switzerland, Bulgaria, Greece, and South America.

THE AMERICAN HUMANE ASSOCIATION

A word should be said about this organization which is steadily becoming a larger factor in the humane work in the United States and Canada, and indeed in all the countries of the New World. Within ten years after Mr. Bergh and Mr. Angell and the Pennsylvania Society had started in their separate fields their varied activities, the need was felt of the opportunity for conference by humane workers generally, and particularly for the purpose of united action in securing proper national legislation. The first meeting for such a purpose was held Oct. 9, 1877, in Cleveland, Ohio. It was at this time and place that the Association was formed. There were present, among others, John G. Shortall, Edwin Lee Brown, and Albert W. Landon, of the Illinois Society, Caroline E. White and Sarah K. Davidson, of the Women's Pennsylvania Society, Jos. L. Smith, of the Cincinnati Society, C. P. Montague, of the Maryland Society,

Abraham Firth, of the Massachusetts Society, and R. R. Herrick, of the Cleveland Society.[1]

The idea of the Association was that of a federation of all the societies of the country whose end was the protection of children and animals from cruelty. It was believed that in an annual gathering of the representatives of these rapidly multiplying bodies there would be furnished the opportunity for the discussion of questions of common interest, and that matters of a national character could be dealt with by such an organization much better than by the local societies.

In one of its pamphlets its objects and methods are set forth in the following words: "The organization, assistance and encouragement of humane societies for the prevention of cruelty, especially cruelty to children and animals"; "The owning, manufacturing, making, publishing, buying, distributing and giving away of humane books, papers, periodicals, tracts, pictures, lantern slides, medals and other things conducive to humane education." It desires it to be understood that its objects are "missionary and educational, and that it seeks in particular not to interfere with or conflict with any local

[1] See annual reports of the American Humane Association.

humane society.   The American Humane Association, being incorporated under United States law, has no jurisdiction for the enforcement of state laws."

Any anti-cruelty society in the land paying ten dollars or over is eligible to membership. Any individual paying five dollars or over is also eligible to a voting membership.

The years that have followed have borne witness to the wisdom of the founders of the Association. From 1877 to the present it has held its yearly convention. Its headquarters are wherever its president resides. At present they are in Albany, N. Y., the residence of the distinguished and widely known humanitarian Dr. William O. Stillman, who has been president since 1905, and who is also president of the Mohawk and Hudson River Humane Society.[1]

[1] Literature and other information with reference to the American Humane Association can be obtained by writing the President of the Association at the above address.

THINGS TO THINK ABOUT

. · .

REFORM IN SLAUGHTER [1]

" Thine is a task of blood: discharge that task
With mercy; let thy victim know
No pain, but let the sudden blow
Bring death, such death as thou wouldst ask."

IT is next to impossible to bring these few pages to an end without a brief reference to one or two subjects that are vitally connected with humane work. Next to humane education, which I think we are all agreed is the transcendent need of the hour, the most important and pressing duty that faces the philozoic societies of our country is to secure the adoption of such humane methods in the slaughter of our food animals as shall reduce their sufferings at the time of death to the minimum.

The cruelties involved in the transportation and slaughter of the more than one hundred millions of animals (not including

[1] See articles on European abattoirs and slaughtering methods abroad by the author in *Our Dumb Animals* for August, September, and October, 1911.

poultry and fish) that are annually killed
for our tables beggar description. Not
only for the sake of the animals, but in the
interests as well of the public health, there
is scarcely a greater reform called for today
than the abolishing of our present ancient
and inhuman methods of slaughter and the
wiping out of the private slaughter-house,
with its unnumbered opportunities for
cruelty and the spread of disease through
utterly unwholesome meat and unsanitary
conditions, and the supplanting of all these
chambers of torture and unlawful traffic in
diseased meat by publicly built and con-
trolled and scientifically managed abattoirs.

Here is the supreme task and duty of
the American humane societies of our
time. We are as far behind such a country as Germany in this respect as bar-
barism is behind civilization.

The larger animals, such as the bullock
and cow, we grant, are generally stunned
either by a blow which shatters the brain,
or in some cases, by a bullet. The bleeding follows while the animal is, of course,
unconscious. But wherever the Jewish
method of slaughter is used, as it is wherever cattle are killed for the Hebrew trade,
the animal is destroyed while in full consciousness and without previous stunning,
by the use of the knife which is drawn
deeply across the throat. Death ensues
at last from loss of blood. This practice

involves much cruelty even before the knife is used.[1]

The animal's feet are first made fast by chains or ropes, then it is thrown heavily to the floor by jerking its feet out from under it, then the head is pried back until the upper part of the face is flat upon the floor, and then the knife opens wide the throat.

With the smaller animals, calves, sheep, and swine, the custom is almost universal among American butchers to kill with the knife without any attempt to render the animal first insensible to pain. So far as I can learn, in some instances calves are stunned before they are bled, but the common practice in small slaughter-houses with calves and sheep and swine is to haul them up by a hind leg, or with calves and sheep to hang their legs, tied together, over a hook and then to cut their throats.

In our great packing houses calves and sheep and swine, herded in their several pens, are one by one jerked up by a chain fastened about a hind ankle, carried, thus suspended, by an overhead device, one after the other, down the line to where the butcher stands. As rapidly as he can thrust his knife into the throat he does

[1] "Humane Slaughtering," a translation by C. Cash, B.A., p. 10.
"Public Abattoirs and Cattle Markets," Oscar Schwarz, M.D., pp. 134 and 143.

his part of the work; on they swing down the line, the blood pouring over face and eyes in blinding flood while they slowly bleed to death, struggling more or less violently with their waning strength.

The explanation of the public indifference to this subject is doubtless to be found in the fact that the slaughter-house and all it stands for is something far removed from our daily life. We never see it. It is seldom called to our attention. Few ever think of visiting it. Here and there will be found a man who, as a boy, followed his curiosity far enough to see some animal butchered, but the chances are that for years he has never given the matter a moment's thought. He sees the meat on his table, but there rises in his mind no picture of the shambles where the floors run red with blood; where men pursue their tasks with hands and clothing crimson-dyed; where cattle, sheep, and swine struggle in the agony of death. The choice steak brings no vision of gaping throat and pleading eyes; the tender chop no suggestion of a lamb hanging by the leg and mutely bleeding to death.

The sights and smells, the filth that is a part of the slaughtering pen, are as unthought-of things as though they pertained to the life of men in the jungles of Africa. And as for women who may be counted upon to champion almost every righteous cause, here is a realm of cruelty they simply cannot enter to see with their own eyes. Few of them could endure the sight. Many a strong man who has forced himself to stand for a single hour amid such scenes, has gone away faint and sick at heart, resolved never to repeat the sad experience.

The supreme goal we ought to set before ourselves as organizations seeking to prevent cruelty is: *The requirement by law that every animal killed for food shall be first rendered unconscious by some method of stunning before the knife is thrust into its throat.*

After the last word is said about the ranchman and the railroad, about the callous drover, the butcher whose hands must drip with blood, the packer who grows rich out of his traffic, — we come face to face with ourselves. But for us there would be no demand and no supply. Upon us, then, no less positively and heavily rests the moral obligation to do the utmost that is within our power to see that these victims of our appetite and desire are slain in what shall be to them as painless and merciful a death as the noblest humanity can devise.[1]

[1] See booklets and papers by the author, entitled "What Some People Eat," "The Testimony of the Camera," "An Indictment of the American Slaughterhouse," and "Interstate Traffic in Calves."

VIVISECTION

We do not forget that it has been defended by men of the highest character — by a Playfair, by a Pasteur. . . . But has not anti-vivisection a case, and a tremendous one?

BRIERLY

WITH reference to this important question, the scientific experimentation upon animals in the interests of medicine and surgery, this at least may be said, that our humane societies are sustained by people maintaining toward this serious subject various attitudes. There are those whose faith in their family physician and in personal friends who are physicians, leads them to say: "This matter I am content to leave in the hands of the physicians themselves. I am willing to trust their judgment, confident that they are faithfully seeking the good of their fellows, that they are humane and worthy of my confidence."

Others say: "This entire field of investigation should be under the supervision of the state. None but the most competent and expert should be entrusted with this right to inflict suffering upon, or to take the life of, any defenseless animal, and at all times the buildings or laboratories where vivisection is practised should be open to the inspection of state officials thoroughly qualified to judge whether the laws with reference to cruelty are being violated or not.''

Still others there are, deeply interested in our cause, who are quite at sea amid the conflicting testimony that they are forced to consider. On the one hand reputable men affirm, and claim to prove, the inestimable advantages that have been derived for man from these experiments; on the other are the assertions of many, also high-minded, sincere people, who deny that any good ever resulted from the subjection of an animal to the experiences of the laboratory.

In addition there is a large body of people, organized into active and aggressive anti-vivisection societies, who are the determined antagonists of the practice in all its forms, denying insistently that any gain for man has ever been derived from vivisection.

With these there are others still who, whether they deny or not that good has come from animal experimentation, believe we have no moral right to inflict pain upon any sentient creature for any purpose or end that is for man's advantage and not the animal's. Independently of the moral question involved, there are also those opposed to vivisection on the ground that, so abhorrent to them is suffering imposed upon the weaker by the stronger, that for no gain to themselves would they have an animal subjected to an experiment that caused it pain.

Besides these there are not a few, admitted in other things to be humane, and who contribute to societies for the prevention of cruelty to animals, who are persuaded that the human race has derived a very positive good from investigations of this character, and are perfectly sincere in defending the practice within what they would call reasonable limits.

Our regular societies for the prevention of cruelty to animals, as a rule, have not entered the controversy, leaving agitation and discussion of this subject largely to organizations making this their special mission.

The Directors of the Massachusetts Society for the Prevention of Cruelty to Animals, though representing various convictions with regard to this important question, have felt themselves warranted, in speaking for the organization, to take the position that all such experimentation upon animal life should be performed only by thoroughly trustworthy experts, and that all places where such experiments are carried on should be open to inspection by such state officials as are *competent* to judge whether the anti-cruelty laws are or are not being violated.

There can be no question that the medical profession must make good its claim, beyond controversy, to have attained by vivisection unmistakable benefits for mankind, or in the end the public conscience will demand its abolition. We believe we may go farther and say that unless this claim can be sustained, the great body of physicians themselves would be among the first to join in the demand.[1]

THE ETHICAL SIDE

When at last in the ever-branching series the complete human being is produced, it knows at once its kinship with all the other forms.

EDWARD CARPENTER

WASHINGTON GLADDEN remarked, years ago, in an address to which I listened, that this whole question of man's relation to the animal world had, so far as he could learn, been left untouched by our writers on ethics. He declared he had searched in vain through all the books

[1] The following quotation from an address made in Boston, March 14, 1912, by President Lowell to the Harvard Club is significant. Speaking of a distinguished physician, he says: "Yet I think I am not mistaken in saying that half of you do not know that his name is Theobald Smith. Now I refer to him because, before he left (for Europe), he told me that he believed more was to be learned today by studying the natural diseases of animals than human diseases artificially induced in them."

on ethics in his library for any recognition of the rights of the lower orders of life.

This, if we remember correctly, was before the publication of "Practical Ethics" by President William DeWitt Hyde, of Bowdoin College, in which our duty to animals, the virtue and reward of kindness to them, and the vice of unkindness with its inevitable penalty are outlined. "Kindness," he says, "recognizes this bond of the kind, or kinship, as far as it extends. Kindness to animals does not go so far as kindness to our fellow-men; because the kinship between animals and man does not extend as far as kinship between man and man. So far as it does extend, however, kindness to animals treats them as we should wish to be treated by a person who had us in his power. Kindness will inflict no needless suffering upon an animal; make no unreasonable requirement of it; expose it to no needless privation."

Frederic Harrison, in an address entitled "The Duties of Man to the Lower Animals," also says:

"I regard man's morality towards the Lower Animals to be a vital, and indeed fundamental part of his morality towards his fellow-men. I refuse to treat it as an extra, an appendix, or finishing touch superadded to our ethical creed. I do so, because I do not know what Ethics can mean, if it be not the due ordering of our own complex nature (a large and indispensable part of which is animal) towards the vast organic world in which we find ourselves." [1]

In the same volume G. W. Foote quotes the following from Schopenhauer:

"The unpardonable forgetfulness in which the lower animals have hitherto been left by the moralists of Europe is well-known. It is pretended that the beasts have no rights. They persuade themselves that our conduct in regard to them has nothing to do with morals, or (to speak the language of their morality) that we have no duties towards animals; a doctrine revolting, gross, and barbarous, peculiar to the west, and having its root in Judaism." [2]

Modern ethical science for the future must surely give larger consideration to this long-neglected field of thought. The bond of kinship between man and the other animals is too close and vital to draw a hard and fast line and say, Here the moral begins and the unmoral ends.

"Evolution," writes so sane, scientific,

[1] "The New Charter," published by the Humanitarian League, London.

[2] "The New Charter," published by the Humanitarian League, London.

and scholarly an author as Brierly, "has lowered our pride of exclusiveness. Our boasted reason is not a monopoly. Ants are reasoners. Bees invented the hive. The new-discovered closer relation is forcing itself into our theology. It troubles it at all points. It is so difficult to define where animal ceases and man begins, why wonder at the difficulty of showing where man ends and God begins? In the question of sin, too, no theologian of the future will be able to discuss the problem without study of the animal consciousness and the unseen something, the sense and volition which guide an animal in life and depart from it at death — what relation has *that* to the unseen something in us which in like manner directs our life and shares this fate of death?" [1]

Men like Romanes shared in thoughts like these. That there is something in the creatures below us that death does not end has been the conviction of not a few of the world's great and good and wise. Such names as Luther, Wesley, Cowper, Southey, Shelley, Keble, Kingsley, Dean Stanley, and Agassiz occur to one as among this number; even Plato is included in them, and Bishop Butler says: "Death removes them from our view. It destroys the sensible proof which we had

---

[1] "Life and the Ideal," J. Brierly, p. 237.

of their being possessed with living powers, but does not appear to afford the least reason to believe that they are then or by that event deprived of them." [1]   To Darwin it was an "intolerable thought" that these creatures with all their capacity for devotion, affection, loyalty, and suffering should suffer total annihilation at death.

There are multitudes, as knowledge of life's mysteries slowly widens,. to whom this thought is also "intolerable." It is incredible to many who have been the recipients, for example, of some dog's unfailing affection, that anything so akin to the love that is at the heart of the universe, can be blotted out. It is a part of the things that are best, and that ought to persist.

The man or woman who has never associated intimately with these lowly friends will not understand it — cannot understand it. Dogs and horses no more than children open their hearts to those who do not love them.

Think of what the following incident means to one who has studied and loved these orders of life below us. Edgar Quinet says that on one occasion, when visiting the lions' cage in the Jardin des

[1] "The Analogy of Religion," chap. I, "Of a Future Life."

Plantes, he observed the lion gently place
his large paw on the forehead of the lioness,
and so they remained grim and still all the
time he was there.   He asked Geoffroy
Saint-Hilaire, who was with him, what it
meant.   "Their lion cub," was the answer,
"died this morning."

Personally, I must frankly say, in face
of the misery, agony, the unrequited,
patient toil, that make up so much of the
lives of my lowlier fellow-creatures, that
unless somehow, somewhere, I believed
there was for these my humble brethren
in the universal kinship of life, an evening
of the scales that deal with the great reali-
ties of right and wrong, my moral nature
could never be at peace.   We work and
hope and trust in the faith of him who says:

> "That nothing walks with aimless feet; ·
> That not one life shall be destroy'd
> Or cast as rubbish to the void,
> When God hath made the pile complete."

BIBLIOGRAPHY

. .

THE first list of books and authors that follows is reproduced from Mr. Henry S. Salt's "Animals' Rights," Macmillan & Co., 1894. He says he has not "attempted to give a complete bibliography of the doctrine of Animals' Rights, but merely a list of the chief English works, touching directly on that subject, which have come within his own notice."

The Fable of the Bees. — By Bernard de Mandeville, 1723.

Free Thoughts upon the Brute Creation. — By John Hildrop, M.A., London, 1742.

A Dissertation on the Duty of Mercy and Sin of Cruelty to Brute Animals. — By Humphrey Primatt, D.D., London, 1776.

Disquisitions on Several Subjects. — By Soame Jenyns, 1782.

Introduction to the Principles of Morals and Legislation. — By Jeremy Bentham, London, 1789 (printed 1780).

The Cry of Nature, or *An Appeal to Mercy and Justice on behalf of the Persecuted Animals.* — By John Oswald, 1791.

A Vindication of the Rights of Brutes. — London, 1792. (Attributed to Thomas Taylor, the Platonist.)

A Philosophical Treatise on Horses, and on the Moral Duties of Man towards the Brute Creation. — By John Lawrence. Two Vols., London, 1796–1798.

On the Conduct of Man to Inferior Animals. — By George Nicholson, Manchester, 1797.

An Essay on Humanity to Animals. — By Thomas Young, Fellow of Trinity College, Cambridge, 1798.

Moral Inquiries on the Situation of Man and Brutes. — By Lewis Gomportz, London, 1824.

Philozoia, or *Moral Reflections on the Actual Condition of the Animal Kingdom, and the Means of Improving the Same.* — By T. Foster, Brussels, 1839.

The Obligation and Extent of Humanity to Brutes, principally considered with Reference to Domesticated Animals. — By W. Youatt, London, 1839.

A Few Notes on Cruelty to Animals. — By Ralph Fletcher, London, 1846.

Some Talk about Animals and their Masters. — By Sir Arthur Helps, London, 1873.

Man and Beast, here and hereafter. — By the Rev. J. G. Wood, London, 1874.

The Rights of an Animal, a New Essay in Ethics. — By Edward Byron Nicholson, M.A., London, 1879.

A Plea for Mercy to Animals. — By J. Macawley, London, 1881.

The Ethics of a Diet, a Catena of Authorities Deprecatory of the Habit of Flesh-eating. — By Howard Williams, M.A., London and Manchester, 1883.

Our Duty to Animals. — By Philip Austin, London, 1885. Argues against animals' rights.

The Duties and the Rights of Man. — By J. B. Austin, 1887.

We add, besides these, the following:

History of European Morals. — By William E. H. Lecky, M.A., 1869. Vol. I, 166, *note* 244, 280, 288, 307. Vol. II, 161, 162, 166, 168, 172.

Humanitarianism: Its General Principles and Progress. — By Henry S. Salt, London, 1893.

Animals' Rights, considered in relation to Social Progress, By Henry S. Salt, New York and London, 1894.

The Place of Animals in Human Thought. — By Contessa Martinengo-Cesaresco, Charles Scribner's Sons, 1909.

Life and the Ideal. — By J. Brierly, London and Boston, 1910, Chapter on Our Poor Relations.

The Humane Movement. — By Roswell C. McCrea, New York, 1910. Prepared on the Henry Bergh Foundation, Columbia University.

The Animals' Cause. — London, 1909.

Manual of Moral and Humane Education. — By Flora Helm Krause, Chicago, 1910.

The Universal Kinship. — By J. Howard Moore, Chicago.

The New Ethics. — By J. Howard Moore, Chicago.

Public Abattoirs and Cattle Markets. — By Oscar Schwarz, M.D., London, 1903.

American Meat. — By Albert Leffingwell, M.D., New York and London, 1910.

a4

257889
HV 4705
R6

Rowley

ImTheStory.com

Personalized Classic Books in many genre's

Unique gift for kids, partners, friends, colleagues

Customize:

- • Character Names
- • Upload your own front/back cover images (optional)
- • Inscribe a personal message/dedication on the
     inside page (optional)

Customize many titles Including
- • Alice in Wonderland
- • Romeo and Juliet
- • The Wizard of Oz
- • A Christmas Carol
- • Dracula
- • Dr. Jekyll & Mr. Hyde
- • And more...

CPSIA information can be obtained at www.ICGtesting.com
Printed in the USA
BVOW11s0440300614

357720BV00020B/580/P

9 781290 728362